HOW TO SPOT INVESTMENT RISK

AUDIOBOOK by Bob Ohneiser, Esq.

Introduction

First - I need to make sure every listener knows that what is included in this book is a personal view of the subject matter without the trappings of a Harvard degree or any certifications to justify your reliance whatsoever. I am not a CPA, CFA nor have I taken any SEC related licensing exams. This is also not a platform for bragging about what I did or did not do. It is true that most of the experience discussed in the book that is about risk, comes from errors I, or others close to me, have made. If you ever meet someone who claims to have a perfect record of investing, run away, as most of what they are willing to share could be described as self aggrandizement and not informative unless you are studying

1

narcissistic behavior. The reason for this book is solely driven by my experience, including observations of others over my lifetime, which leads to my conclusion that the investment system is not balanced, fair or lacking large influencing factors intended to take your savings away. I still invest, but risk is so palpable that some of my best decisions were either hesitating instead of jumping in or waiting to jump in when it seemed the stock was in total disaster mode. I do not need to state the names of very famous individuals who did the "perp walk" and now are serving very long jail terms, as their victims lost most or all of their life savings. If they listened to this audio book, perhaps the con artist would not have succeeded. But then again, part of my experience is precisely rooted in personally being ripped off, as well as watching my father get ripped off by such predators. My father ventured into investing in scotch, realizing as he went to sell it after 16 years of seeing it apparently grow, that all his investment was literally stolen. All the Attorney General in New York at the time would tell us is that it was a scam. My father tried oil leases, gas leases, start-up company investments and even tried raising chinchillas in our basement, only to eventually give them to a local farmer who promised not to slaughter them for their fur. Do not kid yourself. The markets are loaded with predators who would have no problem taking your life savings, while knowing the investment they are pushing will NEVER succeed! Let's not be negative. Let's be analytical, practical and skeptical. Let's learn how to spot the risk instead of being lured by the vision of sugar plums or the house in the Hamptons that the market makers own, while you can't get beyond the gates. Let's get into what makes the markets run so you can be prepared to succeed by not falling for cloaked risks and overstated optimism. There are many terms to understand, so some work is needed. Critical listening is work! If you do not understand the lingo, how can you possibly spot understatements or overstatements that would alert you to avoid the wrong choices? If you are a market maker or already live in the Hamptons, feel free to skip the Background Section. Although I can state that a market maker or NYSA specialist would already be beyond this book I believe the emphasis of this book on improving one's ability to observe and interpret risk could help the experienced investor as well as a novice. This book is trying to quell your fear of the unknown with the knowledge of how to read the so called "tea leaves" to avoid the poisonous brew, while still being brave enough to play the game, hopefully to at least incrementally improve your family's financial future. Be both grateful and optimistic about investing, as many do not even have liquidity to allow them to play the game. As a former NFL Agent, I have seen very wealthy individuals in need of legal aid to get a divorce, after losing all their money to predators both in and outside of the family. Risk is real! It can seem at times, like a devil taking on many forms to lure you into bad situations. Simply put, if you can clearly identify and measure risk, then you can embrace that risk by making sure your upside exceeds it. Imagine the danger in investing your family resources, if you do not really appreciate the risks you are engaging in. Categories covered in this book will be Healthy Skepticism, Background, Risk and Friendship, Nuts and Bolts of Seeing Risk in Financials, Focus on Economic Data, Focus on Chartism, Clichés, Invisible Hand versus Keynes, and Psychology.

HEALTHY SKEPTICISM

Add a VERY healthy heaping of skepticism to everything you hear from the media AND from anyone else, if the communication is intended to lead to an investment decision of any kind. I say that because manipulating the public to stay invested when it should be obvious they should bail is an investment decision. If the executive branch publicizes that there is no need for Ebola virus concerns, for example, while they are quietly stepping up inspections at all international airports, you may be led to stay invested in airline stocks, not realizing what will happen if just a few cases show up at a few airports. How much affect on the markets would you expect if we just had commerce and tourism via airports stop for just one month? Have you considered what could severely affect every one of your investments? Is this why many people just buy S&P funds so they can drink away their sorrows by saying "well - everybody else got hurt by that too"? Well it is not true and it never will be true. Do you really think everybody was hurt by the depression? Can you state emphatically that nobody benefitted from the 911 horror or the bombing of Pearl Harbor? This is just an example to justify a point. I am not suggesting people sit on cash waiting for a major global event to bet on.

Why? The financial markets or at least sectors within the markets are always in turmoil! As an industry where losing is part of the process, the media should be viewed not as a reference desk you find in your local library but rather a public courtyard where some caution is warranted unless you really know the intent of the occupants!

Examples: How often do you hear the statement "Markets down due to profit taking"? REALLY? How do they know that? Have they seen the schedule C's of the sellers long before the sellers even do their taxes?

Do you really think that out of over a billion shares per day all or even most of these trades were at a profit? Isn't the self-serving aspect of these statements obvious? So let's dwell for a moment on the language used by Wall Street to pull you in and keep you in. When you watch CNBC or any other financial networks, you may wish they would challenge the on-air guest to divulge where they are invested themselves or if anyone is funding their appearance. Are you being advised or sold to? Do they ask – "OK so where would you put money to work"? How rarely do you ever hear an emphasis on going to cash rather than changing the mix of investments between bonds and equities, etc.? Given we live in a "free country", did you ever wonder why we can't easily keep our savings accounts in foreign currency? Are we allowed to grow anything on our land as long as that product is legal to consume somewhere on earth? For anyone not sure of this please spend a Sunday afternoon reading the laws we must live within. One of my favorite anecdotes showing how free we are in this country was when I took my aging parents into the entrance to the CIA, driving up to the front entrance to ask if there was a tour they could take of the government campus. You would not believe how many well-armed soldier-types descended on us aggressively, challenging why we drove into the entrance to the CIA. My World War II veteran father actually enjoyed the excitement but I was visibly indignant that Americans would be so rudely met, while asking such a reasonable question. Their fear was palpable making me wonder whether I even understood how hated our society must be that such defensive behavior seemed appropriate. I was warned never to approach the building again but it sure was obvious the organization behind those guards did more and got caught doing more than just gathering intelligence for "POTUS". Keep this in mind when considering stock market volatility.

How often do you hear the TV talking heads say "the fact is" when talking? Are these really truly applicable facts or even facts at all? Or is the person just used to talking at people, due to his or her prior position of power, and unlikely to be challenged by underlings or even reporters while the discussion is on air? This is especially noticeable when a political party or highly partisan investor discusses the options of the day. Listen for the pronouns and lack of corroboration in their contentions. The point is not to merely ridicule but to reduce your risk in investing by not assuming what you just heard was actually a fact, which deserves to be relied upon. What are the real reasons Saudi Arabia is keeping production at a particular level? What is the real cost of our foreign involvement in Afghanistan? Is that country REALLY the only place on earth bad guys could cause harm? How many bridges, dams and buildings are being built? Don't we actually borrow money to "help" foreign sovereignties, yet one will rarely ever hear that on a TV show, typically promoting the policy statements they are fed by our government? Do we even know if these funds are given to foreign entities or are they credits they can use to purchase goods from major political supporters who sell into these markets? (Guns, farming equipment, etc) Should we really respond to seeing wounded children in hospitals as the reason to decide on another 10-year plan without even a question as to authenticity or relevance by the journalist? Do our journalists even know how to ask follow-up questions or are they not allowed to? How much does the USA give, to whom, in what form and most importantly how is it audited before and after the fact? How are such gifts actually given? Do our State Department staff members get wined and dined as they present the check or flown somewhere for the meeting, etc.? Self-serving behavior is what this diatribe is all about. As investors, we need to try to get to the truth of the moment so we can make as careful a decision with our scarce resources as possible. If we knew such funds were not going to be provided, is it possible our friends at the CIA are planning an overthrow which could make us lose all of our investment in that country? Did members of government know about sanctions against Russia before it was announced? Isn't the weakness of the Russian currency easy to predict with such knowledge? Yet as of now, there is no information in the public domain of any such transactions even being investigated. As an investor, it is of paramount importance to try to gauge whether there is a "blood in the streets" moment, where all seems lost, but the ultimate failure is not as probable as the media plays it to be so you can jump into a trade. Is it even conceivable that Mr. Putin would expect us to launch into a nuclear war over their trespass with Ukraine after the red line in Syria bluff? Perhaps you have noticed these non-transparent manipulations and know what I mean but if not, then listen closely the next time a "journalist" makes a statement without demonstrating any proof of why it is a fact or where they got the information from. Is the government actually providing the newscast content versus independent journalism? If so, then how does this affect your investment decision and the risk associated with it? Is your investment about to go up because a new foreign-based order is about to arrive or not? Ask yourself if we have pure journalism and if not, when did it stop? Was it a long time, perhaps back to November 22, 1963 (why were archives closed for any period of time?), or September 11, 2001 (Was there really journalistic coverage of why building 7 fell?) or even recently with the 2008 financial crisis experience as the most recent question mark? If none of these dates even triggered some suspicion, then perhaps you may not have the sufficient degree of skepticism necessary to parse the news and gauge the risk of your pending investments.

Are you listening to a past-based discussion or a future-based discussion? Most likely it is a past-based factor, implying a future-based result you are being convinced to worry about or buy into, etc. First, try to ascertain what timeframe the speaker is using to base the conclusions upon, and then what are the motivations of the speaker. Why is the speaker on TV in the first place? Are they really just volunteering to be on the air or is there an agenda to their appearance similar to why big stars go on late night programs to promote their new role.

Do you really understand the words used in the discussion? Are there other plausible definitions of the words that differ from your interpretation? Are the words chosen pronouns, nouns or overly broad terms like "the market" or "inflation", etc., which you will know when done with this audio book, are defined quite differently now than they were in the past and likely quite differently than what most people think they mean. How do you react when you hear someone say, "The fact is"? Do you know how to "fact check"? Is there any corroborating data to confirm it is likely to be true or not? Another way to think of this is to ask yourself: "OK - if true, what else would happen?" and then check if that is what is happening.

Now let's go through some terms which need to be understood, all of which apply to spotting risk:

BACKGROUND

Who is supposed to monitor accountability in trading - the SEC? Are they really doing it? Does the SEC allow family members of Congressman to trade in the market even if that Congressman is part of a committee reviewing FDA approvals or perhaps new regulations of banks? The more you dig in this area the more you will conclude it is like the wild, wild west when it comes to forcing accountability by the SEC. Nice job if you can get it, but little responsibility for accomplishing the mission. This is the key reason that consideration of corroborating factors must be done before making trading decisions. Didn't we just go through a quite painful experience where most AAA ratings were pure fiction and in some cases purchased ratings? Did anyone notice the SEC held none of the ratings agencies accountable for such violations of our trust? Do your own homework and protect your family assets without looking for fictitious governmental protections to blame for failures.

What does disclosure of financial flaws mean? Is there a restatement that has been made public or is one about to be published? Do the investment bankers and perhaps their families know of an impending problem or just the staff of the SEC or both? How is this managed? How often do you see high volume trading or option activity just before a major announcement yet nobody gets charged for insider trading by the SEC?

Who is held to account for trades made in a particular company? Insiders are a key group to follow and most internet sites show this information on a current basis for free. Unfortunately there is no free publication that shows prospectively what "else" insiders own or what their families own. How much notice do insiders have before an SEC informal investigation or formal investigation ensues? Does the SEC REALLY investigate high volume trades or excessive options activity just prior to a company announcement? Are SEC employees and their families kept in a special IRS investigation category to make sure their non-salary income is reasonable and not trading related? Not likely!

What access to CEO information, which should be considered as "insider", do hedge funds obtain by merely chatting with that CEO? How much information do rating agency staffs have before such events are made "completely" public? Doesn't the FDA know about drug approvals in advance? Is it even possible that over the past year not one employee shared such info? Where was their "perp walk"?

The same is true of investment bankers who are contacted by a CEO asking for help, either to refinance, float a secondary, or perhaps even M&A help. The reason to bring this up is not to castigate all public employees or slam Wall Street, but rather to suggest that in order to gauge risk, one needs to look at what has occurred prior to the news, what happens after the news and how accurate or jaundiced the news was, etc. Never assume you are the only person who knows about something but always assume someone knows more than you do, especially if the company is on a major index!

If you are making a trade and you need it to trigger fast, you would sell at the market, which simply means that you tell your sales agent to take the best price they can but sell it all immediately. In trading terms, this means you are likely to get the bid price assuming there is enough size at the bid to take your shares. The difference between bid and ask when selling or buying is known as the spread. Stocks with less volume of transactions, compared to large company stocks, might have a large change when an "at the market" order comes in. Whereas a Microsoft transaction, by comparison, would likely only have a penny spread. The amount of trading interest at the bid and ask is known as the *size*. This is important to pay attention to if the trade is relatively large for the company stock being traded. This is one of the fundamental weaknesses of putting "stop-loss" orders into the order. If you can remain disciplined during a sale and notice there are only 500 shares at the bid, then you can sell 500 shares and most likely get the bid. The specialist, if it is a New York Stock Exchange traded stock, or the market maker, if NASDAQ, may drop the price he is willing to take if there is no buyer in line for your shares well below the shown bid. So be very careful of dumping a very heavy position with lightly traded stocks. It is always easier to sell into an uptick, which is where the term "selling into good news" comes from. Of course, this implies the sellers had the news before you did and they have already gauged the top of the trading trend. If you book large stop-loss orders in advance on a good until canceled basis, and then the stock gets a large sell order, it could force the stock to drop due to an insufficient size, which then triggers your stop-loss orders, further pushing the price down. Buying while a stock is dropping is known as "trying to catch a falling knife". It is also known as a "value trap", or buying a stock when it was under pressure and it continued to drop after you bought it. If you think a market maker must keep a substantial amount of stock inventory at the bid and ask you would be sadly mistaken. Market makers are profit-based traders not public servants!

Misleading statements intended to make a stock sound great regardless if statements are true or false is called "pumping the stock". "Bashing" is the opposite. It is best to block these messages if you follow your stock on the internet, as all they do is cause unjustified fear or unjustified glee. In some cases, however, these message boards can expose an obscure issue that is actually affecting the stock but it is always critical to remain disciplined in terms of weighing the impact. Anything that impacts the financial viability of a company may already be in the stock value and maybe you are just one of the last people to sell into the bad news or buy into good news. This is one of the key reasons it will reduce your risk in trading to keep a list of stocks to watch before buying any of them so you can test your ability to predict their behavior.

The most watched global dollar denominated commodities moving due to risk, inflation and consumption are gold and oil. No matter what the talking heads say or imply via clichés, very few if any, financial assets rise in a depression. The lack of demand for resources will slow everything, meaning P/E ratios will soften for most stocks as growth is diminishing.

The measure of relative demand at the bid and ask is called MACD. The measure of the amount of shares up or down on a particular day is referred to as "on balance volume". Just be aware that these are backward looking metrics so they may confirm a trend but are not reliable as evidence of an inflection point or trend reversal.

The name of bands that measure of stock performance with predictive criteria is known as "Bollinger bands". This is part of a more complex set of criteria, which is not directly dealt with in this book, as understanding basic market risk is a pre-condition to more complex sets of transaction analysis.

The contract right to buy stock in the future at a specified price usually above current price is a "call".

The contract right to sell a stock in the future at a specified price usually below current price is a "put".

The type of short sale where stock is not actually controlled by the trader is referred to as "naked shorting". This achieved by obtaining the ability to sell a stock without owning it or even paying a brokerage house to borrow the stock for this purpose. These are the types of transactions, including leveraged borrowing or margin deals where one could question whether the SEC wants to regulate the markets or just take credit for having done so in between disasters like in 2008.

A 10Q may be unaudited but the yearly report of company performance that is audited yearly is referred to as a "company 10K". Be very careful of any company, especially foreign ones, that do not provide audited results or perhaps report to their internal taxing authorities different numbers than they present to investors.

A balance sheet measure that shows assets compared to liabilities is referred to as "equity". When you see stockholder equity decreasing over time, one has to question whether management is able to control the destiny of the company or are they sliding toward bankruptcy, etc. In some cases, management may not be adjusting the administrative costs and debt levels as sales slow, which will also be seen in this measurement. Companies who must come to market to sell stock for financing, need to be very carefully studied because dilution of the stock is usually going to push it down.

The income statement measure that shows what customers owe the company is referred to as its "receivables". This is not a big deal for utilities, who will collect what is owed, but if the company you own stock in has a failing product, this number could be more imaginary than real.

The income statement measure that shows if a company is prepared for higher sales is "inventory". If you listen to quarterly conference calls and the CEO calls for greater growth in sales but the inventory of items that go into the final product is not increasing, you may have a problem. Conversely if sales are not growing and inventory is still increasing then that same CEO may be in denial and lower prices may follow to shed the inventory which will lower gross margins, leading analysts to reconsider their evaluation of the company which will drop the stock. This measurement is also valuable to gauge seasonal preparation of a company, such as the Christmas season. Analysts do channel checking to gauge this, which feeds their models to upgrade or downgrade a stock or not. Again, they have much better access to information than a retail investor would.

Another term for a failed reversal is a "head fake". Again, this is talking head verbiage to imply the market is well understood and any turbulence should be viewed as temporary. It also could be hedge funds trying to influence trading action for their own purposes. The point is to take notice of these inflection points to minimize your risk. If you don't know why a stock is acting the way it is perhaps you don't really understand it well enough to trade it. This may be more risk than you should be accepting.

The most untrue statement made by the press explaining a down market day due, would usually report it was due to profit taking. The impression seems to be always pushing that folks who sell are ahead so you too should play the game. The standing joke is that hedge funds sell in May and go away. This is the ever-present fear of brokerage houses. If retail customers were to sell and withdraw their funds, the brokerage house would go away. So one can imagine why no broker ever suggests a customer sell out of all investments, but should rather re-allocate between various financial instruments, as they get a commission on each transaction.

Insider selling is not as meaningful as insider buying but is it possible to tell if the decisions carry a meaning. If a CEO who earns $1 million/year goes on record buying 10,000 shares of his $1/share company, is it really to increase his wealth through long term capital gains or is it a play to send a legally acceptable message to shareholders that they should hold the stock and to perhaps get some added interest in the stock from groups who follow such things? When a relatively low salaried earning CEO buys the stock, which also pays a dividend, it could mean he has confidence in the ongoing results but when they sell, it is always a statement to be studied carefully. Some executives sell stock they received as part of their pay to cover tax liabilities, or at least that is what they usually contend.

Potential violations of covenants will hurt stock values and degrade bond ratings. This gets the shareholder into the weeds of the public reports but nothing brings down a company and its stock value faster than a financial debacle. If the company is required to maintain a certain ratio of cash to debt, etc., it may have to raise cash at an inopportune time to keep from having its bonds called. If the stock is diluted to achieve this, the result is going to be a drop in the value. Insiders such as bond holders or investment bankers dealing with the company will know about these events and information may not be acted upon by them but it has been known to happen where it leaks and somebody takes advantage of it well in advance of the general market awareness. When this type of event occurs as a surprise, analysts tend to shun the stock for a time as well.

The use of cash to acquire outstanding stock instead of other investments is referred to as a "stock buyback". Companies have an authorized amount of stock they can issue. One mathematical way to improve results per share is to increase the numerator of the ratio by greater revenues or profits but at times a CEO may just reduce the denominator to achieve the same result. The same earnings divided by less stock will make the executive seem like he is driving greater earnings but he is just using cash differently than expanding company infrastructure (buy more trucks for a trucking company or more trains for a train company).

A stock that makes a significant change in direction which catches the traders by surprise, may be referred to as a "reversal". Some stocks do this on such a regular basis, they are referred to as being in a "cycle" or "predictable trend". The focus on quarterly results is a good time of year to see this happening, as many traders play the quarter end results but don't want to hold that same stock for the next quarter.

A second guess position for income or timing reasons is referred to as a "hedge". Someone may buy 1000 shares of a stock they are not completely sure is going one way or another, so they may also sell puts at the same price so if the stock drops they can recover some of their investment. This can also be done by putting stop-loss orders in just below the price one bought the stock. This is also dangerous, as at times of softness, the stock may tumble right through those stops, forcing the market maker (if NASDAQ), or specialist (if NYSE), to clear the stops at the market price, which may be quite a bit lower than the stop was set up for. An example of this would be to buy a stock for $100/share and put a stop-loss order at $95. Logically the owner thinks he has protected his down side and can only lose 5%. If the stock drops precipitously one day and perhaps opens at $80, the new owner will get $80 not the $95 he expected. This can also happen if a very large buyer approaches the market maker with an offer to buy at $80 and the market maker takes the order but sells some of his shares into those stop-loss orders to get the large volume order, which will normally put the stock right back to where it was before the large transaction. Except the new buyer who thought he was protected, just lost 20% of his investment. Stop-loss orders don't offer the protection most people think they do. Studying the cost of hedging is a good way to spot the risk of buying the stock in the first place. If there is no derivative/options market for your stock then perhaps its not really going to go up as you think it will. It is a factor to consider when trying to spot risk. Take a look at the pre-market bid for a stock you own to appreciate how low it could open before setting up a stop-loss trigger.

For the fancier transactions whereby one tries to lock in upward and downward action for a set period of time, there are "straddles". The focus of this book is not going to be on esoteric transactions but rather the basics of identifying risk. Given the 2008 timeframe financial system difficulties, it would seem many "experts" could not appreciate the risk of packaging mortgages in such a way that the buyer could not truly assess the risk, while the rating agency was quite comfortable giving everything on paper a AAA (triple A rating). If you can't trust the local rating agency, who can you trust. That is the point isn't it? Volatility seems to be increasing, as is the risk of being in the market.

The media loves to slam those who sell and sometimes label them as having "weak hands". This means that only due to some behavioral weakness would many sell at the same time. Interestingly, those who buy at these times can also be labeled negatively as walking into a "value trap". Something dropping in price does not always a bargain make, regardless if there is no news or just slightly negative news!

Investors love to label everything. In many ways they are like attendees at a race track labeling the horses as being "mudders" or "closers" or "rail riders", etc. The shorts like to insult long shareholders by calling them "bag holders".

On the other hand, people who promote a stock without producing credible facts, are labeled as "pumpers". When these people pump a stock until their rumors cause others to buy the stock, driving the price up, they then sell the stock, making the round trip transaction we know as a "Pump and Dump". This is real. I am not making this stuff up, although it sounds funny to me as I say it.

Many of the shorts will use public media to do everything they can to cause others to feel uncomfortable buying or even holding a stock. These people are known as "bashers". Sometimes a company will expend the management resources to fight off such slanderous attacks but most of the time, these bashers find companies that predictably don't have much public relations muscle.

If enough bad news or false rumors float around long enough, somebody will start to believe a version of them and that is what the short bashers hope for. For the historians among us, its the big lie concept used during World War II, but now focused on enticing people into a stock or scaring them out. Again, we don't see either the Justice Department or the SEC doing very much about these activities.

Bashers will tout the selling by insiders but it is important to distinguish between pre-scheduled selling by insiders and seeing them run to the door because they know something owners wish they knew so they could get out too. It is also important to look at the impact of inside buying. A hundred share purchase by an executive earning a million per year may be a "false flag" move.

The media is pretty strong on making stock owners feel like its never time to sell but it might be time to switch out what you currently own for something else. This is commonly referred to as "rotation".

One of the strangest communications the media tries to feed the innocent owners of stock is the explanation that should there be some sort of major move at the end of a quarter, it is only window dressing rather than somebody who has direct communication with a CEO running for the hills. Analysts have many tools available to them to gauge earnings long before the release.

Apparently, a street-wise investor needs to justify their position at the end of a quarter by selling the stock you own but the clear message is that you don't have to. Just hang in there and wait! The emphasis on balancing between risk assets (equities) and bonds is the message you normally hear.

One of the most redundantly used terms by the media and the salesman in the investment business is to discuss the seemingly magical allocation of their assets. They may say "You should have a 60/40 split under these current market conditions. REALLY? Interesting how getting out of the market completely is never an option, even for a short time. They love to say nobody can time the market. REALLY? Somebody was selling the day before 911 and some of those people had pretty important government jobs. Somebody was selling just before the October 1987 crash and somebody was selling Bear Sterns, etc. just before the Secretary of the Treasury asked for his bazooka worth of bailout funds. Simply put, if you wouldn't buy an asset if you had extra cash at that moment, you probably shouldn't be holding that asset regardless of whether you have a 60/40 or 40/60 allocation.

Another adage Wall Street analysts favor is pushing shareholders to diversify. Theoretically, if one has all their assets in one financial instrument, they have much higher risk than if they have all their assets in 5 financial instruments. If all five stocks are airline stocks, there is obviously more risk than if one is oil, one is a pharmaceutical, one is a power company, one is a bank and one is a real estate investment trust. Carrying it further, there is less risk of losing all ones assets if they have a variety of industries in their basket instead of just one golden egg, unless that golden egg is going to do really well.

The amount of indexes and general economic information one can study is almost limitless, yet most are backward looking. The dry bulk index is a measure of the international movement of goods, as the rail indexes show the movement of goods within the USA. To track such indexes so future trends can be formulated, is a lot of work but will lower one's investment risk.

In addition to measures that reflect the current trends in business, there are many government provided indexes that one can extrapolate the direction the markets will be going. Always remember that if you put all the economists in the world head to foot they would never reach a conclusion. Money supply is a highly touted measurement of the liquidity in the world. Too much money chasing too few goods is the definition of inflation and the reverse would be deflation. A very high money supply figure, which is happening with quantitative easing, at some point will tend to fuel inflation. Money isn't just floating around in the environment but rather is mostly in banks that constantly lend it to each other. In the late 2008 and 2009 period, we heard the term "counterparties" quite often, as banks even lend money overnight for a fee, referred to as the fed funds rate. The Federal Reserve also operates a discount window to help with bank liquidity. As you read about all these terms, which are highly important to the market, try to remember, the Federal Reserve is not part of the US Government and is a 1913 registered business entity! No matter who is talking on TV, you must understand their agendas before listening to anything they say you should do!

We all learned early in school that money is merely a medium of exchange without which we would have to use barter methods to accomplish trade. Well, the world has gotten so small that some traders have figured out how to borrow money in one country in that currency and lend it in another country in another currency. This is referred to as a "carry trade" and was done a lot with Japan, as it seemed its value to the US dollar would not improve and the lending rate in Japan was nearly zero. This is a great example of people not recognizing risk. There may be couple of basis points to be made by borrowing in Japan and lending elsewhere but currency fluctuations can wipe out that basis point in one news story. Would you like to be wiped out by a currency drop due to a Tsunami causing the carry trade to fail while your instinct about the investments you made may have been right all along?

Utilities make for an interesting investment area. They are always willing to cooperate on new ideas that extend their business no matter what it cost for a very big reason. They are managed on a return on asset basis, meaning the more assets they employ to provide power, the more the government will allow them to earn. They are unable to just raise prices as they wish due to their monopolistic power, which comes with a price.

Utilities are touted as extremely low risk (unless one remembers Northeast Utilities when it had nuclear plant problems or Japan Utilities after the tsunami). The lowest risk of any investment is said to be US Treasury Bonds. Given the dollar is dropping in value on a continuous basis, these bonds may not have a big loss risk but they carry a guarantee of losing a little of your assets all the time. The Federal Reserve uses purchases of treasuries as a means of pumping dollars into the money supply and assures the US Government has funds to operate even though they have to pay it back. This adds interest load to the budget and causes a decline in the relative buying power of the US dollar. Please remember that the Federal Reserve was incorporated in

Delaware in 1913 and is not a government entity. At this point, I believe the USA is running over a $trillion per year of excess spending that they have to borrow to manage. Most of the US debt is held by foreign governments like China, who incidentally, has a huge trade imbalance with the USA as well. From an investor perspective, these issues need to be understood and watched, although they don't affect the market on a day to day basis. If a legislator announces he is going to push for a bill to hinder trade with China in a form of protectionism, it is good to understand the real position both countries are in, so the bluff of such a maneuver can be used for strategic investing. Yes, I do believe one can time the market, but it is more likely that all one is doing is trading on better market intelligence, rather than following the newscaster's expression of fear. There are many extremely contradictory government policies that one should understand if they can affect the particular area of the market one is investing in. The USA has been buying the nuclear fuel from the Russians and reselling it to the power companies. So how hard is it to appreciate that at some point, the power companies will be able to buy that same nuclear fuel directly from the Russians? There are a few US companies that depend on such protectionism and when it's gone, so will they be. The same type of dependency risk would apply to companies that depend on import tariffs to create demand, or at least limit supply of competitive products or commodities. These are substantial risks that need to be understood before buying such company stocks. To reduce investment risk, it is important to understand the sources of the company raw materials.

One of the many mysteries in owning stocks is the thought about who else is buying or selling, why are they doing it and how much money is flowing in or out of a stock. This is the stock and trade of market makers and NYSE specialists. It is somewhat measured by a statistic known as "money flow" which basically can show you that a base of interest is forming but the stock has not increased in value. This could just as easily be interpreted as a very large owner releasing his shares in small trades as not to notify the market of why he is selling or that a large owner is selling.

One measure in the overall trading environment that isn't easy to accept is, to what extent is there money flowing into a stock without it just going up? The measurement of money flow does just this. Just because a stock drops in value at the open, for example, does not mean the stock is being sold off but rather that the market maker starts it out at a lower level, mostly to drive his commissions as new buyers rush in for the deal as it appears to be. This allows a measurement of more cash coming into the stock even though the value seems lower or the same. This is worth following and reacting to its messages, as when money is leaving a stock, it is time to consider hitting the exit doors again to lower risk, even if you don't know why.

Some people believe that markets aren't really instantaneous barometers of financial risks but rather some sort of periodic acting entity and therefore they watch and unfortunately abide by moving averages (50 days or 100 days or perhaps 10 days). Most traders watch the market EVERY minute but these folks believe it's all about the seasonal trends. There is some aspect of this that has merit from a risk perspective and that is the quarterly conundrum. Even the great stocks get hit at the end of a quarter, because it is so inexpensive to make trades, why hold a stock after the effect of its quarterly performance is over?

The measurement of unemployment is more about what governmental agencies are going to do than about the number itself. To the extent that political pressure on the Federal Reserve will due to a bad unemployment figure is the issue not what the number is versus the economy. If you are over 50 and out of work you know what I mean. Its not going to be easy to find a job that takes full appreciation of your 30 or so years of experience and if you don't have a safety net, you will spend less money as you look for work. This is a measure of risk when considering that some states have low rates of unemployment and perhaps their municipal bonds are at a much lower risk level than a state with a high unemployment rate.

Whenever I read a report where a point is made, I always look at what is not said by such a statement. This is how I measure disclosure. If a company, by example, says they will meet payroll, then they haven't said they would meet accounts payable or their dividend, etc. Disclosure is an exercise in precise writing to obtain the maximum benefit without making the expected commitment. "We expect to meet our dividend commitments for the balance of the year" means there is a problem with the beginning of next year and dividends will not be increasing this year! Because of the profoundly established temptation to "PUFF one's results" only limited by the veracity of corporate counsel, it is key to study the edges of what is being said.

Wall Street is notorious for many things but one thing everyone would agree to is that they love to label everything even if it is not clearly really definable. Traders often refer to the decision to buy when others appear to be selling as being "contrarian". When considering real factors, this is one of the most overused and misunderstood labels. If gold is going down in price and miners of gold are going down in price, yet someone jumps in to buy the stock of the miners, is it really contrarian or just an attempt to buy low? Is the trader who buys at the end of a very, very bad down day really contrarian or just someone who thinks the market has expended its negative energy and hopes the next morning there will be a bounce even if only a minor one? Frankly, most labels should not even be used unless there is a firm definition all participants can agree on. This is how inexperienced traders get burned. The media says there is no inflation because a particular measurement of inflation approved by the government does not include fuel or food. Does that really mean there isn't too much money chasing too few goods? Does that really mean that the policy of forcing oil companies to add ethanol into their gasoline isn't raising the cost of food for the meat industry perhaps slowing their growth or even putting some out of business? Listening for intentional direction is a critical capability for the successful investor. Watch carefully for conditions or limits to what the CEO says to better understand what the actual risks are.

Another interesting label is the term "capitalism". I am comfortable with the ability to fund a business from equity rather than merely debt or use of government funds but the media treats this term almost as a disease. There are plenty of investment houses that are EXTREMELY profit motivated that are not structured to raise capital through equity and perhaps don't even have debt. There are also plenty of non-profits that are not charitable at all and have executives receiving salaries and fringe benefits that would make a mid-sized for-profit corporation question their validity. I mention these things not out of blatant sarcasm but rather for the investor to consider that to the point that he is acting on news, there might be much greater risk because the words don't really mean what one thinks they mean. Causality is a precious commodity because when one can truly understand what causes their company stock to go up or down then it is more a matter of studying the metrics than guessing how the managers are going to react when things get better or worse. What are your company stock metrics and what variables drive each one? Know this or you may be just guessing when you buy in.

When there are only a few participants in a particular market knowing the metrics is really important as these companies tend to move in lockstep. In an oligopoly, one can price products and provide services with a degree of comfort (less risk) compared to a marketplace where there are far too many competitors to study, meaning any one of them could destabilize the market by one action. Whereas in an oligopoly, they don't really have to do that to thrive. To an extent, the big three auto companies had a nice oligopoly as did the original data providers (WUI, RCS and ITT), but one can see those dynasties do break down when management gets too entrenched or ignore technological advances. The internet ended the record carriers profitability. Japan humbled the big three auto makers by changing the rules on manufacturing which ended the automotive oligopoly. One of the key reasons I endeavored to prepare this audio book was to help novice investors to be able to listen to analysts and stock brokers and the media, without falling prey to their spells. If the result of listening is to either reduce perceived risk of an investment or make one aware it is far more risky than previously thought, then this is progress. The risk to the listener is heightened when he does not realize the speaker is merely handicapping market factors by weighting variables specifically to serve their own purposes. This is not always transparent enough to see it as it happens so in general don't accept what is said without first thinking about what agenda could the speaker have. How many times do we hear a doom and gloom speech from an analyst who doesn't say he is shorting the market before talking? Basically, without some knowledge or market direction at least as it applies to one's holdings or what one plans on holding, is gambling. Would you gamble at a racetrack exclusively by what the guy next to you said you should be betting on? One could make an analogy here about a jockey or horse owner giving you advice in trade for a favor of some sort, compared to relatives of Wall Street Investment house employees taking "advice" and running with it for easy profits, ignoring the pure selfish illegality that it should be labeled as. The negative view on investing is only put in what you can afford to lose. Is that really the basis of why we have 401K's or how our pension plans work? It is merely a way for investment advisors to cope with the reality that their advice just cost you your retirement or your son's education and therefore they shouldn't be held accountable? When their choices do well, one can notice much more bravado than "its not my fault - you shouldn't invest what you can't afford to lose". In order to fairly evaluate risk in the market, one needs to severely consider what the media is saying given their non-admitted bias. You will hear "there is lots of money on the sidelines" as just one example of word play. Obviously, anyone who is on the sidelines is a player and wants to get into the action. Real people on the other hand who don't have all their money in the market have it available for buying furniture, cars, vacations, rent, etc., and it is NOT exclusively waiting for another chance to jump into the market. Did you ever hear any talking head on TV say that its time to take losses? Did you ever hear any of them ever say as the market drops, that its due partially to investors giving up on the market rising and they are taking their losses rather than riding it down?

Why? The prism from which all these guys operate is to entice you to keep all your money in the market all the time. They know there are other options. This is the key reason for the often repeated phrase of "allocation". Did you ever hear them say you should have 60% stocks, 35% bonds and 5% on the sidelines ready to jump on opportunity? Of course, its all about convincing you **not to think** about selling and paying off your mortgage or buying the house next door for rental income, etc. If there is a financial calamity making financial assets perceived at least as extremely risky, then why would ANY instrument based on rule of law and finance be a good choice? What really goes up in a depression? What was Wall Street really afraid of in 2008 and 2009 to drive such extreme action of the US Treasury?

The truest investment statement my dad ever shared with me is that no money is more valuable than having some when nobody else does. Families who did not lose jobs during the depression had a generational opportunity, as others needed to shed assets at any price. Money makes money, and the money, money makes, makes more money! Don't pull the proverbial investment decision trigger until you can view the input being received from the media in a fair, unbiased way! You may get on the same bus as many by buying the S&P Index but not everyone is on that bus.

In addition to carefully considering the always-present bias in financial reporting, consider whether financial tools regularly offered, really offer the degree of risk protection implied. Take the stop-loss tool as one example. If a stock is at $10 and you bought it at $10, perhaps your advisor will suggest a stop-loss order at $9. Even the label of "stop-loss" should be a hint it is a marketing tool as much as a financial tool. Doesn't that sound good: stop-loss? Don't we all want to stop a loss? Now lets take a deeper look at how this tool works. If this stock has a size of 500 shares at the bid and ask at each strike level and normally trades with a spread of 25 cents then it can trade between $9.75 and $10.25 with as little as $4,800 of trading could push the price down and force you out at $9. Now take a look at a scenario where a big buyer comes in to the market maker and offers to buy 10,000 shares at $8.75. The market maker makes money on trading not holding, so he could walk the price down to $8.75 and pick up the order forcing you to sell at $9 or even $8.75 if he chooses to, with the price going right back to $10 a few nanoseconds later. How safe did that feel? Now let's take an extreme case which is probably what you were trying to protect yourself against. The market tanks and the market maker opens that stock up for trading at $6. You don't get $9/share but rather get the closest bid to $9 someone is willing to pay. Are you starting to "GET" the concept that words and labels are intended to convince you of something even if its not absolutely true. Is the "market maker" going to carefully walk the market down, allowing you to get out with your $9 stop or is he going to act in his self interest (generating commissions) and lower the price down to a level there will be active trading, which means he just makes money instead of risking his own money on holding the price up? All these data points are available to your broker, so in order to better understand how risky (how liquid) your intended stock purchase is, please ask him for the size at the bid and ask below the market. If you are buying a 1000 shares of a stock which only has 100 shares of size at the bid or ask, then you are not only risking going above the current ask to get your shares but you will be hard pressed to get your 1000 shares out if needed without taking the stock down a few ticks as well. Obviously, all of this can change overtime but its precisely during moments of downward pressure that the market maker doesn't hold the level with his own inventory, therefore misjudging the size can add considerable risk to your decision. Understanding risk is what this is all about. It's your choice, but wouldn't it be a better choice if you really knew the risks? I've referred to market makers as a general term. These are what the NASDAQ uses. The NYSE (New York Stock Exchange) refers to these jobs a having a set on the exchange and they are "Specialists". The concept is similar in that under normal conditions they manage the market to control volatility, however all bets are off when there is extreme market pressure. They may even stop trading to allow the company to explain what is going on. In a buyout, this could be great for a shareholder but it can be a nightmare when the reason is something like an SEC investigation has begun. Keep in mind, market makers and specialists can move the level of the stock price up or down without volume. This means they don't have to buy stock inventory as it falls or sell their inventory if the stock level is rising quickly. In fact, they have as perfect knowledge about the prospects of a company stock as anyone and perhaps even more than the executives running the company. Do they have friends they talk to? Do they have relatives they talk to? Do they trade information with other specialists while sipping drinks in the Hamptons? How hard is it to say they think the pain is over for a company that has come down or perhaps they really like a new executive for a company they follow and think he/she is done with write-offs, etc.? There is a term that applies far too often. It is called a "value trap". This is where a company may have very good prospects, great income stream, good products and a good balance sheet but it has dropped in value recently so the P/E looks favorable to its comparable stocks. Maybe the dividend rate looks good too. It is a trap in the sense that you may not recognize there are more "shoes to drop". Another cute term for insiders knowing something you don't but other sellers do. In fact sometimes the media accentuates this be producing copy asking how can this stock be so low. It must be ready for a rebound which sucks you into buying it only to find out there is another problem only some knew about. You were trapped because the value was a mirage usually created by the environment. Yes, deception is a real risk and RARELY punished by society in the trading arena.

Unfortunately, it is precisely the need to understand the lingo of the market in order to reduce investment risk. Simple phrases aren't directly convertible. For example, when an analyst describes a company as a "small cap", does it mean the company can't be trusted for its financial reporting because of immaturity or it is too small to be predictable or is it really just a stock that analyst does not follow? Wall Street talking heads are renowned for self-serving comments. Of course, they would have an opinion on a stock but they are too proud to admit they don't cover it. They are too important to cover small companies, which only have about $660 million in capitalization. REALLY? Always remember that the CEO or CFO will take that Wall Street call.

Phrases are often overused to push an agenda rather than be descriptive. How often do you hear "too big to fail" stated as a political comment rather than a financial one? Was GM or GE too big to fail? Of course, any company that lets hundreds of thousands lose their jobs should not fail but should our tax dollars be used to cushion a company whose top executives makes 1000's of times what the basic employee of that company does? As a graduate of General Motors Institute of Technology during the oil embargo, I can tell you first hand how awful top management was and how undeserving they were for getting any governmental benefit. Even today, the effects can still be seen in places like Flint, Michigan, which is a place where members of the board of directors of GM don't live! If only there was more transparency between boards and their CEO pay determination, we would have a wonderful gauge of how a company is being run and therefore how likely our dividend will continue or the stock price will hold up during a general market correction. What we should notice is that most new executives will look to flush out as much risk as possible when they first take over, so the responsibility is put on the prior guy, not on them. It is human nature and most CEO's can be predicted to act in their self-interest at the start of their term. This is often a good sign and it does decrease the risk on the entity stock price going forward, so be patient when a new outside CEO is chosen. The stock may be of a different value than the company for these reasons. You are trading the stock, not the company.

One way to understand the risk in a stock is to look at how the company is leveraged. If you look at a stock like Cisco or Intel, they have little debt to deal with so interest rate changes might affect their product sales but it doesn't directly threaten their ability to service their debt. In many cases, there are covenants on debt that may force the hand of a CEO to do some really bad things to the stock if the interest coverage ratio changes, which needs to be understood. Rather than study the actual bond details, which is what professionals do, one should at least look at the relative leverage a company has to determine the risk of such things happening. On the positive side, a company whose financials are improving will do even better if its leverage is increasing as well. A good example of this is an accretive acquisition, which includes taking on some debt. A company that has a healthy gross profit margin with a relatively low fixed cost basis, including low debt, is far more likely to continue its dividend than one that is living on the edge with high debt. None of this is a guarantee of results but it has a huge affect on the risk level you are undertaking by participating in the market.

If you see a company that has growing income but its administrative costs are growing faster than the sales, ask yourself, "If sales slow, what is the likely decision of the executive"? Will he/she cut this overhead right away or will the balance sheet and cash flow erode first? How much of the sales is repeat business that the company doesn't need to hire new people to obtain? With all due respect to political commentary, business runs on the marginal utility of labor. They are not rewarded by hiring as many people as possible but rather to value each hire as how much MORE is contributed than the incremental cost of that labor. A good example of low risk would be a power company that can sell all its excess power to a nearby community, when the community it is responsible for can't use the power it generated. In power company parlance this is called "wheeling power". It has minimal variable cost but truly is a strength to support the stock. Variable costs tend to move with the top line whereas fixed costs must be covered even if the company sells nothing. High fixed costs or variable costs going up faster than sales are warning signs there are problems meaning there is risk. Imagine a hydro based utility that sells all of its excess power to California where the comparable cost may be nuclear or fossil fuel based.

Rarely is there only one company in any particular business space. This should allow at least a cursory review of the relative financial structure of similarly situated companies. This may not predict whose stock goes up but it does allow a greater understanding of the relative risk of each. Don't ignore the naysayers on a particular stock either. The confidence in any particular stock relates to what multiple over earnings it receives. If the shorts know something that emboldens them to message about it, then smart money is to pay attention. If you look at the entire market over a very long period of time, it doesn't look like anything has stopped its march forward, but if you owned stock in late October 1987 or late 2008 or on 9/11/2001 it didn't feel very good. Rallies and corrections are usually overstated. However, the image of birds jumping off a wire at the same time should be heeded. Nobody on Wall Street wants to be holding long when there is an impending correction. If one jumps. they all jump. The best time to be in cash is when nobody else has any and the prices are falling. Imagine how much wealth was created during the depression by people who kept their jobs and had extra cash to buy todays "nifty fifty", when they were only pennies per share. Did we ever hear of the SEC checking on short sellers just before September 11? What possible reason would they not have done that? What about December 7, 1941?

Of course the future isn't clear, but consider that company executives receive calls from large investment houses who check inventory levels and predict earnings on a regular basis. Even if a company does well, it will be punished in its stock price if the earnings fail to meet investor expectations. It will really be punished if the executives don't somehow warn the analysts bad news is coming. They don't like to be proven wrong! It is always a very curious observation to see large volumes just before a well-respected analyst changes their view of a stock, yet they are not supposed to share such changes with their internal brokers prior to releasing it. Ask yourself: if you were in the same position and you were about to really slam a company, seriously challenging their ability to perform, would you not help your investment house customers to get out before you release the downgrade? We all assume that nobody can front run the news but history is replete with examples of how it's done and how often it's done. The language of analysts may seem cryptic at times but it can be deciphered. What do they mean when they say perhaps the market can "melt up" or we should "expect some retracement" or "no major catalysts are on the horizon". The trend is your friend so all they have to convey is the direction without ever mentioning any particular stock. All of this language must be considered when you try to reduce your risk or at least be aware of risk as it changes.

Risk is often observed offshore too. Some seem to think the entire earth is guided by the Dow Jones Industrial Index (average of 30 Dow stocks which changes from time to time). There are other indexes and it is a continuous discussion on which one, if any leads another. Here are some of them:

- Brazil is represented by the Bovespa Index of about 50 stocks traded on the Sao Paolo Stock, Mercantile and Future Index.
- China is represented by the Shanghai Composite, a capitalization-weighted index that tracks all shares on the Shanghai Stock Exchange.
- Germany is represented by DAX, a stock index representing 30 of the largest, most liquid German companies that trade on the Frankfurt Exchange.

- Japan is represented by NIKKEI 225, a price weighted index comprised of Japan's top 225 companies on the Tokyo Stock Exchange.

There are other exchanges and indexes but considering this audio book is intended to help individuals seeking to spot risk, it seems contrary to the goal to start educating the listener to exchanges in third world countries or specialized indexes. Although one of my best investments ever came from the Russian stock market (RTS), but that was extremely risky, especially at the time, thanks to Mr. Yeltsin. The recent turmoil in the Ukraine with economic sanction saber rattling has impacted the RTS and indirectly other exchanges as well. No exchange is an island!

RISK and FRIENDSHIP

Friends may frequently tell you about ideas they can't defend. When it involves money, it is a temptation to allow yourself to be drawn into investing with them. I've been drawn into such ventures as well. It may seem comforting at first to be investing jointly with a friend. It reminds me of the old adage "misery loves company". Imagine how silly you will feel to find out your friend only bought 100 shares of the stock of the century he was touting that you put your life savings into. How about finding out he/she sold it right after you bought it and never told you while you watched your money disappear? Does he/she explain in enough detail what the risks are or just tout the upside?

The best advice for these situations is to readily offer to put the company on your watch list and do just that. Analyze how it acts and whether or not you can predict its movement, given what the rest of the universe is doing. If your friend is an insider, then its a much more serious issue that you don't get such advice in an evidentiary way. If your friend is an executive for a FEDEX-type company and he says at a Christmas party that the level of deliveries is incredible and way above prior years, you might want to check it out but it does not really reduce the risk that the numbers that come out at the end of that quarter confirm his view and are above analyst expectations.

When a friend makes a suggestion, do you really discuss his commitment to tell you prior to him selling or under what conditions could the whole thing backfire? Investing is a process that you have to be comfortable with and be prepared to pay a heavy price for short cuts. Risk is real and a real effort must be expended to at least try to minimize it. Ask anyone who recently got laid off:

when did they realize the company was failing? No doubt they will be quite negative, but it's highly doubtful they sold their company stock in advance of that layoff. If you work in an investment firm approached by that same company CEO who is about to lay off employees but is trying to do a refinancing in advance, do you really think neither you or any member of your family or ring of contacts will be buying that stock anytime soon? Perhaps even the reverse will happen but I would hope that temptation never occurred to you unless you already have an estate in the Hamptons with other Wall Streeters. Do any of these folks check with the SEC to make sure they know the rules in advance or is that really necessary? Perhaps with this small example of the flow of information, it will be obvious how little we know as retail investors compared to Wall Street especially when they are directly in the acquisition and divestiture loop. Wouldn't it be nice to have perfect information just once in a lifetime of investing?

NUTS AND BOLTS OF SEEING RISK IN FINANCIALS

Let's go through some simple processes one can do to see if obvious risk is present. Most of this information is both free on the internet and readily available. Reducing risk is the best one can do. No belief is justified that results in both eliminating risk and still providing for a return on investment. Even Treasury Bonds don't guarantee that when you get your dollars back they won't be worth less than you started with! All we can do is improve the odds. Yes, that does sound like a gambling term and it is intended to, as dealing with unknowns is gambling.

Here are some categories to accomplish this:

1.   What are insiders doing? Are they controlling their destiny or reacting to it?

2.   Will company have to dilute its equity to raise funds soon or at all?

3. Are the message boards full of fraud-type accusations about the company? Has the SEC initiated an inquiry or worse, an investigation?

4.   What is the relationship between sales and fixed costs? Is the CEO managing a tight ship or filling the building with his friends even if the cash flow does not support it?

5.   Do you understand what business this company is in and what the likely future is for it? What future environment will uniquely benefit this company? (Obviously, a new health care law will make some companies winners and others losers just as a recent example)

6. What drives the dividend policy and has the company lived by it? Is there a written commitment or at least a long history of regular dividends and hopefully a record of increasing the dividend while they expect to have the cash flow to sustain it?

7. What has the history of stockholder equity been?

8. What percent of the outstanding shares are controlled by institutions/insiders?

9. What are the analyst estimates in the future and how often have they been missed?

10. How does the trailing versus projected P/E differ and why?

11. What is the relationship between earnings per share and dividends paid per share? Do the products or services have price stability or perhaps growth?

12. What is the trend of relative indebtedness? Is long term debt coming due soon at higher interest rate levels? Are there

severe business impacting covenants if the company delays any payments?

13.   Are company press releases pumping futures or just stating facts? This is an especially sensitive item in biotech companies.

14.   Listen to at least one quarterly conference call to gauge how the executives grasp the business and how transparently they respond to questions from the investment community.

15.   How is the CEO paid? Does his employment contract include a change of ownership clause?

16.   Does the CEO have a golden parachute or perhaps gets all his options converted upon a change in ownership?

17. What is the premium on the "at the money" calls? What can you tentatively conclude by a premium or lack of one? These are added data points to give you greater feel for what is really going on which in turn does reduce trading risk. Always check this

premium before buying a stock that has options!

18. What is the premium on the "out of the money" calls over what time period?

19. Is there any premium for "in the money calls"?

20. What does the relative volume look like in the stock over the near term versus the long term and what direction has that volume caused the stock to go in?

21. What part of the federal government regulates the company and what is that relationship like? Do you expect this relationship to change and why?

22. Can you hear the agenda in these terms? Reversing gains, taking profits, corrections are healthy, classic rotation, raise cash to pay tax on profits.

LET'S FOCUS ON ECONOMIC DATA

1. How is inflation really measured? Why doesn't it include food and oil? What message is intended as legislators say on TV

there is no inflation when food, gas and even tolls are going up much more than the stated inflation rate? Do bedtime stories ring a bell?

2. Is unemployment really at the level the government tells us it is? If you are over 50, try to find a job.

3. What assumptions go into debt measurement? Does the government regularly report what we already owe which is only around $19 trillion in 2014 or do they warn us of the almost $100 trillion that it will grow to if we meet our future commitments already committed? Would you be very inclined to support new overseas government projects if you knew that your grandchildren may already have a yearly tax burden multiple times the level you pay now? Is there any doubt that the current key to paying back all the dollars of debt is to pay

such prior higher value dollars with future lesser value dollars?

4.   Underneath all investment is the value of the currency the investment is made in. If the dollar drops in relative buying power by 5% per year and your annuity pays you 3% per year, you have guaranteed your family they will have less assets every year at the rate of losing 2% per year. Most economic discussions ignore this underlying feature but it is real. Try traveling overseas to a country that has not been diluting its currency and see how far your dollars go. Can you remember the days when hard currency was treated differently than soft currency? Currency used to be backed by gold, which because of its physical limitation tended to hold the currency values stable or at least expose politicians who tried to weaken it. Perhaps the only way to maintain your families' assets at its current value is to

properly invest it, earning more than the inflation rate and the dilution of the dollar rate.

LET'S FOCUS ON CHARTISM

Regardless how you view Chartism, the fact that such a large number of investors follow chartism means you have to at least acknowledge it and perhaps, at times even benefit by it. Those who follow the charts will trade based on their beliefs and even if a minority of trades are done this way, it will amount to an effect. Chartists will move the market both in a day and for a trend. Sometimes it sounds like handicapping a horse race when listening to a chartist on TV, as they always have a reason to worry, to be optimistic and always can explain what happened on a rear view basis.

Knowing the charts is not the same as knowing what the CEO is going to do because he/she explained it to you in your Wall Street Investment Banking office. Some designs do deserve observation. A flag formation can be interpreted as a long-term avoidance of the stock by institutions or the company is indeed going out of business but for chartists it represents an opportunity. The slightest positive news may force the shorts to cover and given the pressure on the stock from such prolonged downdraft, the upswing could be quite rewarding to the astute chartist and for you, if you notice it as well. This is a critical time to listen to the quarterly conference calls, especially to how the CEO answers questions from the analysts. If one analyst changes their view, it is worth much more in terms of directional change than a whole raft of retail investors and can happen minutes after the conference call. I have been amazed by CEO apparent nervousness on these calls, including stuttering and sluggish responses by executives making enormous salaries. This is a very important way to gauge the real risk of your investments, as it tends to open up serious issues Wall Street has with the company and by logical extension, with the stock.

Have you heard these clichés recently?

- Do not be afraid to add when a stock drops
- This looks to be the beginning of a healthy pullback
- Worst-case scenario is already in the valuations
- It makes sense to participate because you can't time the market
- You can't time the bottom
- Volatility is the price of admission
- Catch a bid

INVISIBLE HAND VERSUS KEYNES

These concepts are often bantered about by TV talking heads, which you need to understand. It is hard to imagine that there was ever a time when markets, especially the stock market, were ever truly free from interference by a large entity. In my lifetime, we've seen people try to corner the market, trade in advance of terrorist events, rumors, FDA approvals or denials affect the market, etc.

If anything resembles the invisible hand it would apply to our expectations of government regulation toward fairness. Unfortunately government actions ALWAYS come with an agenda which is rarely if ever directly and only geared to helping investors. Even the ROTH IRA which is touted as a gift to investors basically forces an investor to cough up a lifetime of gains in their IRA to pay taxes and then they can receive the benefits of the ROTH IRA. A detailed future cash flow analysis would show that this is pure folly unless you knew for sure you were going to earn a lot on investments over a very long lifetime and have a much higher tax rate in your later years than the year you flushed all that IRA money in front of the IRS who gratefully would take a big share upfront. There is value in noticing that appropriate government action should occur and it doesn't. Recently we saw a spate of companies that were being propped up by federal donation, only to then go bankrupt. One would expect these federal entities to apologize for wasting tax dollars or at least fire the individuals who released such funds in what I would contend is an ultra virus way. There are many examples where such funding has even continued well after the entity goes bankrupt, which for investors should be a very valuable data point. The current "Keynes type influence" is not profit, growth, employment or even infrastructure-driven. Social agenda has taken a lead role in utilizing centralized tax dollar control, not business. Apparently, the old adage that what is good for business is good for America is no longer valid.

When politics prevails in borrowing into what seems to be a high government debt environment to give money to troubled foreign entities and dying businesses, it is a major data point for investors to consider when adapting to what risks this behavior creates. Will the dollar really go up organically when the USA seems to be driving toward being such a huge debtor nation? It may rise on a comparable basis as our military might is still pre-eminent and money does look for safety in times of global peril but that is not long usually term. If the USA has to pay more over time to borrow money to operate in this open checkbook environment, it should color our view of various risks. Will gold really drop below its equivalent value relating back to when the dollar was gold backed? Will our international exporters continue to do well as the dollar drop keeps them competitive against other currencies and global competitors? Will global financial risk be driven by large entities taking carry trade risk to jump on currency volatility and if not bailed out when they make the wrong bet break the system? I am not suggesting you worry so much you fail to make your money work for you but don't fall asleep assuming the rest of the world has permanently accepted the current world order, especially when our country seems to be paralyzed in political bickering. Trading in the markets is a worldwide activity, so even if Americans think they understand why the USA is doing something overseas, it does not guarantee the rest of the world may have the same conclusion, as they may not be watching the same channel on TV we are.

The next obvious affect on risk is perceptions of an election shift in power both overseas and domestically. Desperate people do desperate things and absolute power corrupts absolutely. If the unemployment rate is of highest import, what level of debt will a desperate politician vote for just to get re-elected? Can the USA sustain its debt level if the almost $20 trillion was under a TIPS basis instead of a fixed, artificially low rate? TIPS are inflation adjusted treasuries, meaning that if the US Government has to pay more to borrow money at the same time inflation is soaring, the cost to taxpayers could accelerate into unachievable levels. A downgrade of the quality of American debt is a BIG RISK to market level maintenance. Just consider how much it will cost 200 million American taxpayers if the interest payment to China's ownership of $1 trillion of US debt alone goes to 8%. It would be about $24 per American taxpayer per day just for China and about $484/day per taxpayer to pay for current debt levels. Can anyone imagine just how worthless the US dollar would have to be to allow the working Americans to sustain such a liability in what would then be current dollars? Wouldn't you like to have owned gold and oil stocks (dollar denominated commodities) as this happened? Well, it is already happening - just to a much lesser extent! Imagine how much of your income will be paid under a progressive income tax system if the dollar is worth another 80% less over the next decade. Fixed income retirees, unemployed and very low income individuals will have a much lessened quality of life than today. This is an analysis of how to observe risk not a political tutorial. While most of this might turn our stomachs as Americans, we need to carefully understand what is really happening in the world which we can't control. Our family assets will suffer the consequences, or hopefully survive, if we better understand such palpable risks. This information may not be easy to listen to but for those of us who have had family that lived through the depression, this isn't the worst you have ever heard. Will social security really be able to adjust to such inflationary pressures our national debt will unquestionably force? Will our children and grandchildren really be able to sustain the longer living baby boomer generation in a manner in which they expect to be accustomed?

How will local government entities finance their infrastructure needs if their bonds no longer have federal tax exemption privileges? How do local teacher pension programs afford their actuarial responsibilities with low interest bonds? Given that federal tax rates for individuals are more likely to increase, both on an absolute basis and also because of a diluting dollar, aren't municipal bond funds even more valuable and riskless than previously thought? If the federal government stops new bonds from having such privilege, wouldn't the previously issued bonds jump in value? The federal government forces savers to withdraw funds from their tax free accounts at certain ages that could be lowered if funds were needed, which will even further exacerbate the tax consequences of getting older, while trying to both live and take care of children, etc. What do you tell your children to do with their extra cash knowing they are highly unlikely to ever get social security to any significant extent?

These concepts need to be appreciated by investors, as real world issues diverge considerably from what the media covers and even when the media covers such issues, there are palpable agendas quite apparent, which may cause investors to make the wrong decisions. The USA can't import its way to prosperity and create jobs at the same time. Export companies will fight against a stronger dollar. A sharply rising treasury rate will affect third world country ability to get funding and, of course, the stock market will react as perceived less risk assets can create income. Our government gave money to GM as part of the bailout and taxpayers were rewarded by jobs moving overseas by GM. What do you think companies do with funds held overseas they can't merely wire transfer back to the USA without major tax consequences? Have our tax policies lost sight of underlying relationships between the purpose of the tax and the result of the tax being collected? A road tax that fixes the road is what makes sense but a road tax that ends up being paid to Pakistan as a gift, does not. This type of inconsistency creates risk from an investors' perspective, as it clouds the impact of government in our Keynes-type view, versus a free market mentioned earlier. The lack of clarity of government policy and inconsistency increases risk as the future becomes more unclear.   For the truly wealthy, their funds move more to avoid risk than to create income. If your family had a $billion you would understand this. They are extra territorial and more concerned about succession and security than P/E ratios. How many times did we hear TV commentators promote buying BRIC country assets (Brazil,

Russia, India and China) without a real analysis of the country and currency risks underlying these suggestions? The same inability to honestly examine not just what can happen in the future but how quickly it can happen, is what you accept as risk by following such suggestions without truly understanding the mosaic that is foreign investing, even if the company stock is on a major exchange. Perhaps its what they don't say that will be of the most importance for you to truly gauge the risk but don't expect the journalists to ever pick up on what is not said or what major issue is near the edge of what is said. The best way to consider the risks of following such suggestions is to test whether corroborating signs are clear or not. This requires homework both in advance of such input and certainly after such input. Having a manageable list of stocks or bonds you are watching is the starting point because over time you will be able to test such hypotheses as frequently as needed. For example, when the tsunami hit the nuclear plants in Japan, it was obvious the suppliers of enriched uranium to Japan would drop as well. Only by having had such companies on your watch list could you possible tell if their drop was overdone or not. In these cases, a well understood market forecast would allow you to jump into a dropping favorite (catch a falling knife) where the general market risk is pushing for a larger drop than your greater knowledge would justify. This is a good example of embracing risk, as your understanding can justify the additional fortitude needed to do such things. If you knew that Casualty Insurer X was not affected by hurricane Katrina but its stockwent down along with other companies that were affected you might have an interesting opportunity. Yes - the very fact that a huge hurricane all but broke casualty companies the risk that it affected company X is near zero if you did your homework correctly. Now once the claims are done being responded to most similarly situated casualty insurance companies will be raising their fees to customers. Since this business is an oligopoly it should be expected that participant will match such rate hikes rather than go for new customers by price reductions. A recent fallacy one could notice is the push for a pipeline from Canada to the ports of New Orleans at the same time Congress lifted the ban on exporting fuel from the USA. Knowing we don't have any new or expanded refineries underway in the USA, how would this increase in supply make the USA more energy independent?

These comments are meant to challenge your willingness to enhance your listening capability as part of the investing homework not to make political comments. Exogenous variables can affect your investments and may be the best tools to justify delaying or at least considering the timing of a trade. For any fact to be ascertained as true or not, one must find multiple sources and multiple companies, which should be affected by such a fact, to be at least somewhat comfortable the fact is really a fact. Sometimes a solid fact has a delayed but causal affect. Hurricanes which are initially disastrous to casualty insurers, can be a real boon to the ones not affected by the current disaster and usually the rates for such protection increase after disasters. So profitability in the next year may be much better, especially if no major disasters occur.

PSYCHOLOGY

Do we act differently when faced with a winning situation or a losing situation? The double down is sometimes used in the investing world but it is definitely used in the gambling world. If you own a stock that has gone down from when you bought it why do you stick with it and what would make you buy more of that stock now that it is lower than when you bought it initially. Some analysts will refer to this thought process as just lowering the basis or "if you liked it at $10/share you must love it at $5/share". You don't gain or lose until you sell a stock so even if it is lower than you originally paid you haven't really lost the money yet. Why not sell it and take you loss? Are you afraid to lose money you knew was at risk when you originally invested it? If that same stock were 20% higher than when you bought it how hard would it be to sell it compared to deciding to take a loss? In accounting terms such a reduced value could be referred to as "sunk cost". Is it possible that you indeed have a delusional view of your prowess in selecting stocks and by not selling it when down you are protecting that self serving label? What makes the most sense is to make sure your self awareness is intact and you understand what variables have changed which caused the stock to drop. This honest self awareness will serve you well when investing under the least risk possible. Psychologists tell us that when it comes to taking personal risk humans tend to take far more risk to avoid a penalty than to benefit from an advantage. This means we can sell a stock when we are making money far easier and willing to take much less risk than selling a stock that is at a loss. We tend to take much greater risks to avoid a loss. Being aware of this should help you reduce your investment risk as you will now recognize that perhaps if the sale you are considering is not being made or you are buying more of a stock while it is down you might be acting irrationally. There are many real world (non-investment) examples of this behavior. Could President Nixon or his chief counsel avoided great personal loss had they come clean as soon as they were made aware of what had gone on apparently without their pre-approval but once they avoided coming clean and apparently started participating in what was charged as obstruction of justice they lost more. The risk was not reasonable but to avoid any loss they took extreme risk. Gamblers regularly double down to get their money back even though they should know the risk is significantly heightened by this type of behavior. Know yourself so you can know your investment risk clearly!

CONCLUSION

Risk is relative but once an investor can imagine the gut-wrenching feeling of losing all of their family resources, the focus on understanding or at least recognizing risk takes on an appropriate value. I sincerely hope this book helps to do that. Awareness is an open-eyes and open ears activity. Investing goes well beyond the "trust but verify" dictum. "Never trust without corroborating proof" would be more appropriate. The time to think about what is making you buy or sell is before you buy or sell. Risk needs to be uppermost in your mind NOT profit. The profit may be an illusion or worse. It might be adding more dollars to a bad decision rather than taking a loss as I discussed in the psychology section. Investing is not like gambling where you have a substantially neutral dealer giving you the cards. Almost everyone who you come in contact with including hearing or seeing on TV have an agenda which might be contrary to your best interest. Understanding risk and frankly embracing it when there seems to be an opportunity is the key to doing well four your family in the investment world. Fisherman who venture into the open seas pay attention to weather forecasts and don't rely on tourist-based weather comments. So why would you invest by following the advice of strangers, especially those who don't disclose if they have an agenda or not. "Pushing one's own book" is a phrase you hear once in a while which refers to a talking head who is not telling what he or she believes is happening as much as trying to get you to buy something they already own or sell something they have already shorted. It is highly manipulative and predatory. Welcome to Wall Street!

www.ingramcontent.com/pod-product-compliance
Lightning Source LLC
Chambersburg PA
CBHW071228170526
45165CB00003B/1040